I0473129

Legal

ALL RIGHTS RESERVED.
No part of this book may be reproduced or transmitted in any form whatsoever, electronic, or mechanical, including photocopying, recording, printing or by any informational storage or retrieval system without express writer, dated and signed permission from the author.

About The Author

 Kenneth J. Wynn (Ken) studies business trends and teaches people how to earn profit by offering strategic insight and techniques on how to maintain multiple streams of income.

Ken has built large network marketing organizations with businesses in over 40 states and 6 countries. Ken has spoken and trained network marketers in Canada, El Salvador, Peru, Ecuador, Panama and the United States. He has addressed over 10,000 people during business conventions.

Ken has been in Information Technology for 25 years and has focused on healthcare system integration the last 20 years. He received his B.A. in Economics from the University of Maryland, College Park.

After getting his start in Information Systems at the U.S Department of Agriculture, he moved on to Philadelphia, PA to work for Sprint as a regional data analyst managing data for 6 offices.

A move to Miami got him started in healthcare when he worked for a medical dispensing device startup company. He currently does private teaching on web site design as well as work with students on high school/college retention issues.

Ken currently lives in Miami, Florida and communicates daily with his daughter and son. Ken enjoys reading, music, currency trading and sharing ideas with friends and family. In the late afternoon you can find him at the coffee shop on 125th and Biscayne!

His passion is transferring knowledge to anyone who is willing to be teachable. His first computer was a Radio Shack

Tandy 1000ex with a 300 baud modem, things have changed! One of his favorite quotes is "**You can put up with any what, if you have a big enough why**".

Ken can be reached at 305-432-2787 and ceo@kenjwynn.com.

INTRODUCTION

Let's talk about fear for a moment. Part of the process of network marketing is doing things that you have never done before. Traditionally, as a networker, you are asked to do certain activities to drum up business and build your network. We will talk about them now because they are what usually drive people out of the business as soon as they get in.

Cold contacts –

One of the biggest fears people have is making contacts. The traditional networking model deems "everyone is a possible business partner". You have been told that the waitress at the diner, the guy at the post office and the successful lawyer who lives in your subdivision will all make good business partners. You are told that you will never verify that until you contact them about your business. Contact them. Are you kidding? That means you actually have to have a conversation with them about business. That means telling the successful lawyer that you have something that will make her more successful.

Here's a reality that you already know. You are not comfortable doing this thing called contacting. Contacting is a skill. Even though you have read some literature on contacting and you have practiced; you don't want to contact anybody! Why? The simple answer is fear of rejection. Nobody wants to be rejected at any level. The fear of rejection alone has made millions of people make a quick exit out of the network marketing business. You will soon learn how to work with that fear and be successful. Just so you know, everybody at every level of business has some degree of fear of rejection. That's the good news. That means you are like everyone else. Those people in your organization above you have succeeded with fear. If they can do it, you can do it too. Your secret weapon will help you.

Phone calls –

Most of us spend a significant amount of time on the phone daily. We talk to friends, family, colleagues and others. You are now involved in network marketing. You are asked to call your friends and invite them to look at your model. What just happened to the phone? It now weighs 300 pounds and has spikes coming out of the earpiece. Network marketing has turned an everyday common piece of equipment into something that makes you sweat. Sound familiar?

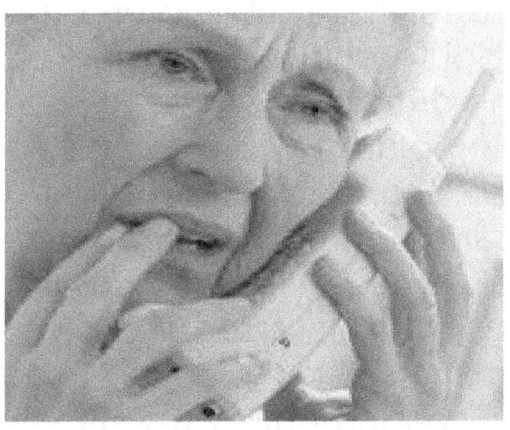

This is another fear you will learn how to work through once you enlist your secret weapon. No matter how many phone scripts you learn and practice, there will always be a certain element of fear. Help is on the way!

Presentations –

I remember my first network marketing presentation. Yes, I have been involved in this great industry for over 15 years. It was a guy named Eric Brown and he worked in the information systems office at a hospital. We met for lunch. I was prepared for my first one on one. I brought different colored markers to show the different income levels in the marketing plan. Even though I had practiced, fear set in during my presentation and something happened that I have never seen again since that meeting. Sweat started shooting out of my palms. It literally looked like a small fountain coming out of my hands.

I was so nervous that I moved my hands over the paper and my multi colored presentation became a mixed shaded blur. I got mixed up and realized I had lost Eric when he leaned back, crossed his arms and just nodded repeatedly as I tried to recover. Did Eric join my network? I am sure he was sitting there thinking; "are those the best colors to use?". He did not join. Once I learned to use my secret weapon, presentations got easier. I ended up doing hotel meetings in front of large groups. I even had the privilege to speak in front of over 10,000 people on two occasions. Will you have to do that in order to build a successful network marketing business? The answer is no of course. I know many people who have built substantial incomes in total obscurity. They just learned how to use that secret weapon to their advantage.

Sales –

Did you know you are in the sales business? Despite what you may have heard; products must be sold in order to generate income. Of course this is based on a product based model. There are other models that deal with information and technology as well. Guess what; either way, you are in the selling business. You are not "sharing" products with people. You are convincing people that the value of the items you represent are better than your competitors. Fear of selling is real like most fears people have building their network marketing business. You will soon learn how your secret weapon will help generate sales and income.

There are a number of other fears and headaches associated with building a successful network marketing business. There are a number of fears and headaches associated with building any successful business. That's just how life works. The difference is that when you build a traditional business, you don't have a secret weapon. You are on your own. That is a lonely way to make a living and that is why most people decide to be happy with a job and never seek out the great wealth building opportunities abound.

97 % of people who get involved in a network marketing business never create significant income. In fact, statistics show that over 90 % of network marketers never get their business out of the red. These statistics are grim. With numbers like that against you, why would you want to do this? The opportunity to become financially free is a big incentive. ***You will never get rich working for someone else***. That thought alone used to keep me up at night. The thought of trading time for money and living paycheck to paycheck was something that haunted me.

If that thought haunts you as well and you still want a shot at economic freedom, let's get started on 10 steps to network marketing success. Your secret weapon is waiting.

Step 1 - What is the best network marketing program for you?

Are you currently in a network marketing program that is not a real good fit for you? That is a question you must answer. If you haven't signed up for a program already, you need to learn how to evaluate the programs to see what you will need to be successful

1. Company profile - There are thousands of network marketing programs available to you. They range from energy drinks to cars. If there is a market for it, rest assured there is a network marketing channel to support that business. There are the big ones that have been around for 30 years or more; Amway, Shaklee, NuSkin. When

researching a program, you need to do a quick company profile.

How long have they been in operation?

Approximately how many people are involved in their program?

How does the compensation plan work?

How is the company perceived in the public?

How are the products perceived in the market?

The longevity of a network marketing company is very important. If the company has been around for a while, there is a good chance that they are doing something right. One of the problems associated with network marketing is, here today, gone tomorrow. Some companies only use the network marketing channel to make a few bucks. This leaves associates out in the cold; which gives this model a bad taste in their mouths. I would recommend you don't get involved with any network marketing company that is less than 20 years old. 20 years is a good bench mark. It means the company has weathered some economic storms which mean they have staying power. A stable company is important. How many people are associated with the company is important too.

Does the company have an army of motivated people moving their products or services? It is important that there are many people on the team. If a company has less than 500,000 members, I would avoid them. There is no such thing as market saturation. There is plenty of room for everybody to succeed. Strong numbers represent strong belief in the company and product line.

The compensation plan is at the core of the network marketing business model. How does the company's compensation plan work? If you can't understand it, how will others that you bring in understand it? The compensation plan should be simple, include a generous bonus structure and possibly have a pass down structure in place. ***It should not make you pay a monthly fee for a website***. That is an indicator that the company may not be financially strong and may not be around next year. Many short-termers subsidize their compensation plan with the old $24.99 monthly hosting fee for your site. With hosting and domains being offered at $2.99 a month, do the math. Nothing is more frustrating than watching people waste their hard earned money. Incentive is a great motivator. The compensation plan should include bonuses and incentives for performance. That means making sales! If the compensation plan doesn't reward overachievers, it probably won't be around long. Does your business die if you pass on? If you owned a brick and mortar business, you would probably have someone to keep it going without you. It would be great if the network marketing plan allowed you to pass on the business to a survivor in the family. There are a few that do. Those are the ones that are in business to help you create long-term wealth. Seek them out!

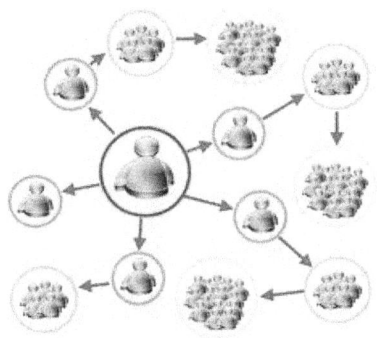

Perception is reality, right? How is the company perceived in public? That will be important in the beginning, but not so important once you understand how to use your secret weapon. The big companies have all had public opinion issues over the years. Amway was the "soap" company. Now they have thousands of products and thousands of companies linked up with them. They even own a NBA team named the Orlando Magic. Shaklee was the "vitamin" company. Now they have various products added to their line. The same can be said about NuSkin and Herbal Life. The one thing each of these companies has in common is their ability to adjust and change with market demands. Those are the companies that you want to partner with. ***Change is the only thing that is constant in***

this world. Partner with a company that can handle that.

Products are important. Don't let anyone try to convince you that it is the relationships that matter the most. If products are not positioned correctly for the market, you will be on the losing proposition of the business. You will be on the losing end because you will be the only one purchasing them. If no one is buying, stop the bleeding and move on. Are the products too expensive? If you ask that question while viewing the marketing plan, then guess what your prospect will ask? Here is one from experience. If the company has only one product, don't waste your time. People are always looking for the new wonder drink or pill. That means you will be constantly replacing people because

they are looking at that magic bullet
from the next company.

Step 2 - Set some goals

You have evaluated the companies and have chosen one. Now it is time to change your thinking and begin the process of creating wealth. By changing your thinking, I am referring to doing something only a small percentage of the population does. That of course is setting goals. When you create written goals, you put your brain in motion. The human brain is a goal seeking machine. Those who are wealthy understand this concept. Only 5 % of the population set goals and write them down. Is it coincidental that 5% of the population control 95% of the wealth in the world? The rest of those non goal setters actually work for them! ***If you don't have goals, you will always work for someone who does.***

Most people are taught to think big. Set big goals and chase them with passion is what you hear in the network marketing world. Another take on that is to have dreams that take your breath away. ***These two phrases are ingredients for failure!*** Learn how to take small steps and succeed. Let me repeat that another way. Focused thinking with a plan of action that creates incremental successes will keep you in the game long enough to impact your financial position. I am an advocate of 1, 5, 10 and 20 year goals. We all need a path to follow long term. But, in terms of winning in network marketing, you must laser focus your goals to 1 month increments. Trust me on this and you will see the results you want. Don't believe you are going to make $100,000 your first year. In fact, don't start looking at six figures until around the third or fourth year. I am just being realistic. And yes, you have probably been told not to be realistic. Be a dreamer instead, right? That's why only 3% of network marketers ever create real residual income. Those are the people who are planted in realism and working on a structured plan. I would rather see someone set a goal to read 1 book on sales and marketing each month instead of attending some rah rah meeting. More on that later.

There are plenty of books out there on goal setting. Buy them, and then read them. ***Focused goal setting is a down payment on your future***. The more focused, the better. Your upline support team should be able to help you. They know what you should expect regarding how your business will grow. They have already walked that path and will help you stay planted. Sit down with your support team and have them set monthly goals for you. Here is where their knowledge and experience will help you begin to squash your fears.

If you have a plan of action, you basically know what to expect. That will make you more comfortable with the process. Most people get involved in network with the idea that they can do it on their own. Failure is assured when you take that approach.

Introducing your secret weapon.

There is someone in your organization who has demonstrated absolute success with the business model. This person is probably talked about every time the marketing plan is discussed. They are touted as the person you need to meet. ***They are your secret weapon***. Here is one question that you must ask anyone who is trying to recruit you into their networking organization. That question is "who is in your immediate upline that is making a medium six figure income that you can introduce me to"? When I say medium, I mean $300,000 per year or more. This is the magic question that will determine whether you create success or just become another network marketing tragedy. Think about this question for a moment. What you are asking is this: who has the sales experience and knowledge that I can learn from without investing a large amount of time and money. What do I mean when I say invest a large amount of time and money? If your secret weapon lives on the other side of the country; you really don't have proper access to them. Your secret weapon must be local because you are going to live at their doorstep until they help you become successful.

Here is the network marketing missing link which keeps 97% of networkers out of the economic winners circle. ***Most, if not all networkers never get the information on how to build their business from the right person***. How can someone who just got started 2 months ago lead you down the path of success?

If you are going to succeed in network marketing, please walk through the rest of the steps understanding that you will only learn from the one with the track record. Your secret weapon is the person who is making that 6 figure income. That 6 figure can only be generated two ways. First, they must be very exhausted selling products to people. Or second, they have taught some people the principles they have learned and those people are successful. Yes, duplication is the key to success. Unfortunately you can't duplicate what is not duplicable. Your immediate upline sponsor has nothing to teach you about creating wealth. Does that sound too strong? If you are serious about getting into the game and becoming a real player, you need to understand that principle. Yes, it is a principle. It is a bad principle that so many networkers fail by. ***Most new networkers see their immediate upline as the experts. This just isn't true. Therefore, the ego of the immediate sponsor gets stroked and both remain broke***.

A smart businessperson will get their colleagues to the best information. Once they learn this, their business will take off. Your secret weapon is waiting to be put into action if they are committed to their team. Just so you understand something very important about network marketing so you won't be disillusioned; ***network marketing is work***. Even the folks at the top are working hard if the organization is to remain successful. That image of you sitting on the beach six months a year and receiving huge residual checks is just that; a dream. I have personally spent time with one of the biggest networkers in the world. He works his business about 320 days a year. And yes, he is a billionaire. He continues to be a secret weapon to hundreds personally because he understands the principles behind network marketing.

So, let's get through the rest of the steps with our secret weapon. You will learn how to build your business successfully if you use your secret weapon in each of the remaining steps.

You now know how important using your secret weapon is in your business. If you have no one in your area that meets the requirements of the secret weapon as described above; I would not join that organization. You would be simply wasting your time.

Step 3 - Who do you want to be in business with you? Aka, make a list.

Many network marketing teams want you to make a list of everyone you know. Why do they say that? The logical answer of course is that you don't know if they are looking for an opportunity until you ask them. Or, they say they don't know they are looking for an opportunity until you show them. People, network marketing is not a life boat or the answer to the poor's economic problem. Unfortunately, most people are taught to reduce their business to that level from the very beginning with the list.

Here is the problem with the list. Most people only put names on the list that they think need the business opportunity. Understand, your immediate upline will tell you to put everybody on the list that you know. ***Fear causes selective listening!*** The list is very important to a certain point when you are first getting started. Your list will help build a team if you use your secret weapon. Here is how you do it.

As stated earlier, your qualified upline has built a large business. They understand the importance of this activity. They will help you if you make a list of everyone you know and then take that list to them. Let me repeat this another way. Write down a list of everyone you know. Starting out with the most successful people you know. ***<u>The good news is you don't have to worry about calling them</u>***. Feel better? Take the list to your secret weapon and have them go through it with you. Let them know who you think the possible players are. Make sure they have current calling information. Now here is where the fun begins and you start to see the power of the secret weapon. You are going to ask them to do two things regarding this step.

Number one; you are going to ask them to give you the best title of a book used to learn how to make cold contacts. Then you are going to give them your list with the potential players highlighted and then ask them to call those people to see if they are interested in the opportunity. If your secret weapon is truly committed to you and their organization, they will handle it. They may ask you to send them a brief email letting them know a good friend will be calling them about a project you are excited about. Make sure you use the words your secret weapon wants you to use. The pain of list making is no longer going to stall you out of the gate. Doesn't that sound great? Fear removed from an important process. Let's move on to the next step in our process.

Step 4 - Make some new friends

Cold contacting scares you to the hilt, right? It did me until I learned to use my secret weapon. How much would you learn if you had your secret weapon show you how they meet people? I did not say meet people for business. Too many networkers make the networking business a full-time job with overtime _**in their heads**_. You don't have to think you have to approach everybody you see as a business prospect. In other words, I am giving you permission to relax and lower the fangs that stereotypes have been given to networkers. The good news is that you have that recommended book we talked about in the last chapter, right. You understand that natural communication will take you further than prepared speeches that people can read right through. Now, back to our secret weapon and how they will help you.

Ask your secret weapon when will they have 1 hour to spend with you. You basically want to see how they interact with people in a natural environment. You want to see their body language, words used and general reactions to people. That 1 hour could be worth a million dollars to you. Now, if that is true; and it is, then how many hours do you want with your secret weapon? Believe me, if you show that you are serious and will do what is necessary to succeed, your secret weapon will work with you.

There is no fear involved in learning how to meet new people. Not only will books teach you skills on contacting people face to face, other resources such as the Internet are available as well. Please understand that you are in business. Most network marketers never get past amateur status. That is because they will not tool themselves as professionals do. Contacting and cold-calling are skills. Skills can be learned. That's why they are skills. ***Professionals acquire skills to help them maximize their opportunities***. 97% of networkers never do that. Am I getting your attention? We don't need any more casualties in the network marketing industry.

Step 5 - how do I expose this business?

One of the dumbest statements you will here in network marketing is this; "the business is not your business until you start doing your own marketing plan presentations". Why do I call this dumb? Nothing will scare a network newbie out of the network marketing business faster than telling them they have to do something they fear more than death! Yes, ***people fear public speaking more than death***. Here is what you need to do to build your business with meetings. Use your secret weapon. There are two things you need to do.

Number one, ask your secret weapon what is the best book out there that teaches people how to speak effectively in public. Number two, take each person who is interested in the marketing plan to your secret weapon. Are you bugging your successful secret weapon? Not if you are in this business to win and not just kicking the tires. While you are reading and learning how to speak effectively in public, you are leveraging your time and growing your business. By the way, you are also expanding the business of your secret weapon. And believe me, they like that. Are you starting to understand this strategy? Maybe it will jump right out at you in step 6.

Step 6 - What did they just see?

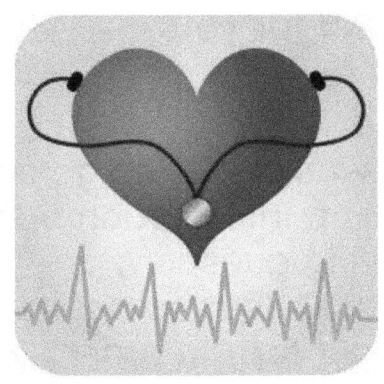

One of the biggest fears networkers have is the fear of rejection. One of the biggest fears human beings have is the fear of rejection! Everyone has heard about the prettiest girl in town who never went to her prom. She was never asked because all the guys didn't want to get rejected by her. There are millions of dollars of presentation follow up material out there that was never picked up by the network marketer. Secret weapon to the rescue. There is a book that your secret weapon will recommend to you. I will give you the title now. It is called "How to Win Friends and Influence People" by Dale

Carnegie. While you are learning the skill of communicating with people, you are going to use your secret weapon to close the deal for you.

How great would it be to go and get your follow-up information and not have to ask that big question; are you ready to get started? Your secret weapon has already asked for the order! Here is the good news about your secret weapon. ***They already know the psychology of the positive command brain***. Translation, they know how much people hate saying no, similar to rejection. That means you will not be going to pick up your follow-up materials with your tail between your legs. You will be going to fill out the paperwork to start a new team member.

Step 7 - Keeping score

Let's go back to goals. They say a soldier in the midst of battle doesn't know if they are winning or losing. Remember when we talked about setting those monthly goals? Well, once a month you are going to sit down with your secret weapon and tally up your successes. This counseling session is a necessary part of your development.

They will want to know your progress on the recommended readings as well as other things in your life. Building a solid, honest relationship with this person is vital to your long term success in the network marketing business. ***You are an asset to your secret weapon***. In fact, you are a franchisee in their franchise. Once you are moving up in income, you will see how much you mean to them. This is a business. The counseling session is an open evaluation of your performance. You are paid through activity of product/service movement. Learn to take advice from them and move on it. ***They will never give you bad advice. It is not logical if you think about it. They understand the principle of helping people get what they want so they, in turn, will get what they want. Zig Ziglar.***

Now, I want to touch upon something that is related and very important about the use of your secret weapon. I have not talked about your direct sponsor very much. If they are smart, they have read this book and applying the principles. I need to touch upon this because it does happen in the network marketing business. If you become tight with your secret weapon, you will have success. You will build a network of people. There are some people who will try to knock you out of business because they know all of those people in your network will move up to them. This is called blowing someone out of the business. The good news is that it is not a regular occurrence. But, there are some mean people out there who would love to lazily profit from you and your secret weapons hard work.

Step 8 - Joan Kroc is living proof that it works

Ray Kroc and Dave Thomas are no longer with us. Their legacy is important to network marketing and the success regular people have created. The franchise model that parallels network marketing is based on something that most people don't understand. McDonalds, Wendy's and the other franchise businesses have a secret weapon just like you do. In fact, it is the same secret weapon which I have described throughout this book.

The secret weapon is a system that ties all of the operations together. When you buy a franchise, you are buying a system that will literally guarantee your success. You can probably count on one hand the number of McDonalds that have closed in your lifetime. I personally have not seen one.

Your secret weapon will put you into a training system that each network marketing company uses. You need to acquire new skills. You need to learn how to sell, learn how to contact, learn how to present and finally, learn how to teach. If you are going to have success in network marketing, you have to master these skills. You are going to need time to learn these new skills. That is why your secret weapon is so important. Your secret weapon will give you the time needed to learn and help build your business at the same time. The books you will be recommended to read are a part of the training system. Spending time with your secret weapon is another part of the training system.

As you develop the skills that will help you develop a significant income, your secret weapon will be there for you. The goal is that eventually you will become someone's secret weapon. This will take some time. This is not a 1-2 year process. For most people, this process will probably take 3-5 years. I hope this doesn't disappoint you. Remember, we are not looking for people who want to kick tires and search for something for nothing. The world is full of those whiners. Most secret weapons are looking for mature adults who are willing to understand that business is a process. Only success that happens overnight is usually a lottery win. Most lottery winners file for bankruptcy after 5 years. Why? They did not have a system to **grow through** to prepare them for the income.

Step 9 - These products are cool

You will need to learn and use the products you are promoting through your network marketing program. If you don't use the products, neither will your team members or customers. Income is made in business when products and services are exchanged for currency. That means you are in the sales business. Learn to get good at retailing products. The most successful network marketers will tell you that sometime in their career; they learned that selling products was pretty lucrative. Your secret weapon will be more than happy to teach you methods to create a large retail operation.

Step 10 – Don't Let Anybody Take This Away From You

When a pit-bull bites down on something, it is very hard to shake them lose. Commit to your secret weapon and your business in a similar fashion. There are going to be people out there who will tell you everything from "only the few at the top make money" to "I've got a basement full of products I couldn't sell". Remember back in chapter 1 when I said this business is not for everybody? Well, it isn't.

Network marketing is for anybody who is trainable, ambitious, open-minded and committed to improving their financial status. Network marketing is based on principles. One of the biggest being; "if you help enough people get some things, you will get some things as well". A win/win business model like network marketing is proven. That is why hundreds, if not thousands open up every day.

The important thing is **_you really have nothing to fear if you use your secret weapon_**. There is a secret weapon in every successful organization. Your job, should you accept it, will be to build a solid, long term relationship with that person. They will be sincerely interested in your success. Your success is their success and that is what the network marketing business model will always promote. Hang in there, read, listen and become a professional by using your secret weapon. May you have all the success you are willing to work for. GOOD LUCK!

Bonus Section – What is Network Marketing, really?

For those who are just beginning to get tired of the trading time for money rat race; here is a special excerpt from a book I wrote a few years ago. I think the message will speak for itself.

There's a story about a village that needed fresh water brought in from the river every day. Two friends started the daily process of carrying buckets of water back and forth to the village. One of the friends had an idea. His idea was to create a pipeline that would move the water to the village center.

He approached his friend with the idea, knowing it would be *extra work without income for a period of time*. They would have to work overtime without seeing any result up front for a while. His friend thought about it and could not see how the pipeline would pay off. He declined the offer and went ahead about his daily work of carrying buckets for the daily pay of $2.00. His friend, we will call him Matthew, decided to build the pipeline.

Matthew carried buckets during the day and worked on his pipeline at night. Though it was hard work, he realized that his vision for the future would help him make it through. He had a goal.

He wrote that goal down and kept it in his pocket so he could see it.

He would pull out the goal and read it when the sun was getting too hot to move in the afternoon. He would take it out and read it aloud when he was carrying those last buckets before he would start his nightly work on the pipeline. He would read it out loud before he would go to bed knowing that it would not be long before he would have to get up and begin carrying the buckets. He would read it after taking his weekly wage and buying more tools for his pipeline, an investment he understood was a part of the process.

Meanwhile his friend, let's call him Evan, enjoyed spending his money and treating his other friends to a good time each night. He enjoyed the immediate gratification of the income. In his mind he felt that the town would always need water, therefore, they would always need the water he carried in the buckets. As time went on, Evan found it harder to maintain his pace of carrying buckets. The town's elders began to see him slowing down, producing, and carrying less.

Matthew was energized by his dream and goal of finishing the pipeline.

The pipeline was completed in 5 years. The pipeline did exactly what Matthew envisioned it would. It created an automated source of water for the village. It also did something more important than that. It created an automated source of income for Matthew. The goal and the  vision of the future became the present for Matthew. Matthew became the wealthiest man in the town through his pipeline.

Because of his knowledge and hard work, Matthew began creating pipelines in other villages. He then began to franchise his technology out to other people. He received a portion of every gallon of water that ran through each of his pipelines.

Pop Quiz: What is this called?

-Passive residual income.

How does the story end? Matthew took his idea for building pipelines to his best friend Evan. Evan was immediately let go by the town once the pipeline was flowing to the town center. There was no longer a need for a bucket carrier. Matthew offered Evan a partnership in his pipeline business. Unfortunately, Evan had no vision and could only see value in trading time for money.

Years later he came back to Matthew and Matthew gave him a job as a driver for one of his regional Presidents. He eventually retired and lived his days with family who supported him.

What do Jay-Z, Michael Dell, Bill Gates and Russell Simmons have in common? They are modern day pipeline builders.

They all had the vision and the dream to put themselves in a position to create residual income that continues to grow every day. It doesn't matter what industry, pipelines can be built if you are willing to set a goal, set a plan of action, and take massive action. That is what those guys and others like Oprah Winfrey did.

Passive Income

Evan was a slave to a paycheck. He traded time for money and would spend his life looking for the next job as technology continued to change. He enjoyed the short term pleasure of making income and spending it at nice restaurants with his other friends. His physical constraints finally caught up with him and he could not command the same income as before.

Matthew learned the principles of delayed gratification and investment. He invested his time and money into building his pipeline. He had the discipline to look past the immediate and build his future. By doing so, he never had to worry about income again because he understood how to build income through pipelines.

The Moral of the Story:

If you are just getting started in the working world, you are already aware of what your choices are. As stated earlier, you will need to continue to retool yourself as you move from job to job. Learning personality identification will give you an advantage in the job market. Here's an alternative. Find something you love to do and use it to create a pipeline while you are working for someone else.

How great could it be to have an independent income coming in that matches your salary in 5 to 10 years?

Give yourself some options while you are still young. By the way, if you are a seasoned employee and you are reading this, you still have time to build your pipeline.

What do you love to do and what are you good at? If you  have great math skills, create a product that you can sell on how to solve math equations. Do you have a special talent on growing roses? Why not publish an eBook on how your secret technique will bring amazing results to their gardens.

I have chosen building websites and promoting digital products as my pipeline. I enjoy researching and finding markets where there is a need for a product and low competition supplying it. This is called niche marketing. I have been involved in this business for a few years now and I'm having fun building pipelines.

Remember, there is no limit to where your brain can take you once you begin to start looking at ways to build pipelines.

It's a fun process and you can do it.

You can reach me at:
CEO@kenjwynn.com – 754-800-5549

Here's a list of resources that have helped me in my network marketing career. Please consult with your secret weapon about these resources before you use them. They are very powerful.

As a Man Thinketh -
http://nbiznow.com/downloads/asamanthinketh.pdf

The Strangest Secret Audio –
http://nbiznow.com/downloads/tss.mp3

Think and Grow Rich audio -
http://nbiznow.com/downloads/tag
r.mp3

The Richest Man in Babylon -
http://nbiznow.com/downloads/trm
ib.pdf

The Richest Man in Babylon (Audio)
http://nbiznow.com/downloads/trm
ibmp3.mp3

Here are a couple of programs I
endorse because they really work!
Get them and share them with
your team.

How to build a business with cold
leads:
http://nbiznow.com/network-
builder

How to Add 10-30 people into your
network per week.

http://nbiznow.com/network-
academy

www.ingramcontent.com/pod-product-compliance
Lightning Source LLC
Chambersburg PA
CBHW071637170526
45166CB00003B/1356